Read Together

Hello, Reader!

This year you will read many wonderful stories. In this first book, you will meet a cuddly cat on a mat and a playful pig in a wig. You will read about a fox that gets fooled and a busy bug in his new little hut.

Are you ready? Here We Go!

HOUGHTON MIFFLIN

Reading

Here We Go!

Senior Authors
J. David Cooper
John J. Pikulski

Authors
Patricia A. Ackerman
Kathryn H. Au
David J. Chard
Gilbert G. Garcia
Claude N. Goldenberg
Marjorie Y. Lipson
Susan E. Page
Shane Templeton
Sheila W. Valencia
MaryEllen Vogt

Consultants
Linda H. Butler
Linnea C. Ehri
Carla B. Ford

 HOUGHTON MIFFLIN   BOSTON • MORRIS PLAINS, NJ

California • Colorado • Georgia • Illinois • New Jersey • Texas

Cover and title page photography by Tony Scarpetta.

Cover illustration by Nadine Bernard Westcott.

Acknowledgments begin on page 263.

Printed in the U.S.A.

ISBN: 0-618-25777-2

10 DW 11 10 09 08 07 06 05 04

All Together Now 12

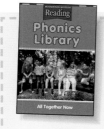

Big Book: **Ten Dogs in the Window**
by Claire Masurel
illustrated by Pamela Paparone
Bank Street College Best Children's
Books of the Year

realistic
fiction

realistic fiction

nonfiction

Phonics Library:
Nan Cat
Fat Cat
Tap Tap

4

On My Way
Practice Readers

Cat
by Alice Lisson

Fan Cat Can Jump
by Iris Littleman

One Big Hit
by Kathryn Lewis

Theme Paperbacks

Bear Play
by Miela Ford

Dan and Dan
by Marcia Leonard
photographs by
Dorothy Handelman

I Had a
Hippopotamus
by Hector Viveros Lee
CCBC "Choices"

Surprise! 128

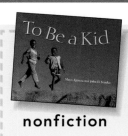

Dot Fox
*by Denise Zimmer
illustrated by Dominic Catalano*

Dot Fox got a wig.

fantasy

realistic fiction

fantasy

Big Book: Jasper's Beanstalk
*by Nick Butterworth and
Mick Inkpen*

Best Books for Children
United Kingdom Children's Book Award

fantasy

fantasy

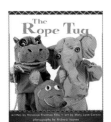

play

**Phonics Library:
The Bug Kit
Quit It, Zig!
Rug Tug**

On My Way Practice Readers

Five Big Boxes
by Irma Singer

The Pet
by Maria Cara

Where Is Tug Bug?
by Oscar Gake

Theme Paperbacks

"What Is That?" Said the Cat
by Grace Maccarone
illustrated by Jeffrey Scherer

The Pet Vet
by Marcia Leonard
photographs by
Dorothy Handelman

Spots
by Marcia Leonard
photographs by
Dorothy Handelman

To read about more good books, go to Education Place.

www.eduplace.com/kids

This Internet reading incentive program provides thousands of titles for children to read.

www.bookadventure.org

All Together Now

Teacher
Read Aloud

Because we do
All things together
All things improve,
Even weather.

**from the poem
"Together"
by Paul Engle**

The Cat Sat

Words to Know

go   cat
on   Sam
the   sat

Sam Cat sat.

Go, Sam Cat!

Sam Cat sat on the .

girl

Lynn Munsinger

The Cat Sat

written and illustrated
by Lynn Munsinger

Sam Cat sat.

Go, Sam Cat!

Sam Cat sat.

Go, Sam Cat!

Sam Cat sat.

Go, Sam Cat!

Sam Cat sat on the .
girl

25

Think About the Story

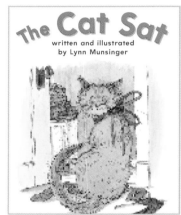

1 Why did the girl say, "Go, Sam Cat"?

2 What was the best place for the cat to sit?

3 How would you get the cat to move?

Write a Label

Draw and label a picture of the cat. Share your picture.

27

The Mat

The Mat
by Nadine Bernard Westcott

Words to Know

go   Cam

on   cat

the   mat

          sat

Cam Cat sat.

Cam Cat sat on the mat.

Go, Cam Cat!

Nadine Bernard Westcott

The Mat

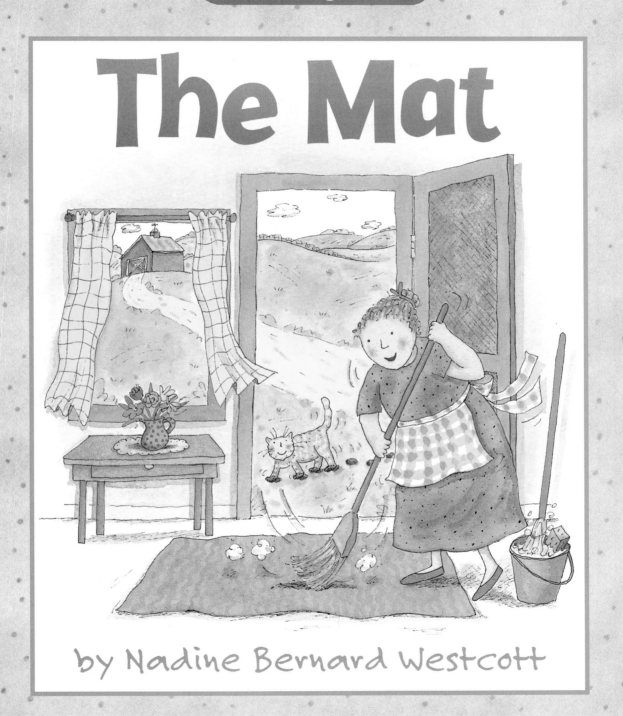

by Nadine Bernard Westcott

Cam Cat sat on the mat.

33

Cat, Cat, Cat! Go, Cam Cat!

 Cow **sat.**

 **sat.**
Goat

37

 **sat.**

Dog

38

Cam Cat sat.

Go!

Cam Cat!

The mat sat on Cam Cat.

Think About the Story

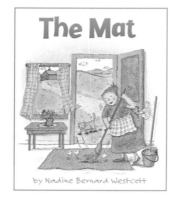

The Mat
by Nadine Bernard Westcott

1 Why do you think the animals sat on the mat?

2 Why did the woman yell, "Go"?

3 Would you want animals in your house? Why?

Write a Sign

Make a sign to help keep the animals out of the house.

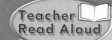

Cats

Cats are furry, cats are small
Cats are hardly big at all
Cats can purr and cats can mew
Do you like cats?
I sure do!

by Jacquiline Kirk, Age 9
Mauritius, Indian Ocean

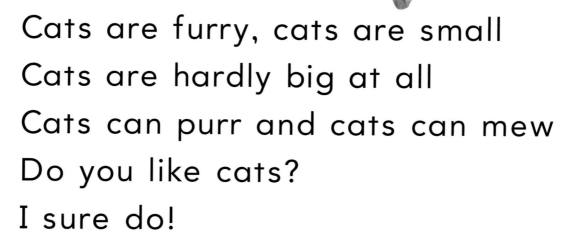

At Night

When night is dark
my cat is wise
to light the lanterns
in his eyes.

by Aileen Fisher

Nan and Fan

illustrated by Lisa Campbell Ernst

Words to Know

not	Fan
jump	can
here	pat
and	fat
Nan	

Nan can jump.
Fan can not.

Nan and Fan can go here.

Nan can pat the fat cat.

Meet the Illustrator
Lisa Campbell Ernst

Nan and Fan

illustrated by Lisa Campbell Ernst

Nan can go.

Fan can not.

Nan can jump.
Tap, tap, tap.

Fan can not.

Nan can pat the fat, fat cat.
Pat, pat, pat.

Fan can not.

Nan can go.

Fan can not.

Fan, Fan, Fan!

Go, Fan!

Nan can go.

Fan can go.

Think About the Story

illustrated by Lisa Campbell Ernst

1 Why did Fan follow Nan?

2 Why can't Fan go to Nan's school?

3 What would you do if a pet followed you to school?

Write a List

Make a class list of pets. Write "Our Pets" at the top of the list.

We Can!

written by Diane Hoyt-Goldsmith
photographs by Joel Benjamin

Words to Know

and	fan
here	Nat
too	Pam
we	Pat
can	

Pam can fan.

Pam and Pat can fan.

Nat can fan here, too.
We can fan!

Meet the Author

Diane
Hoyt-Goldsmith

Meet the Photographer

Joel Benjamin

68

We Can!

written by Diane Hoyt-Goldsmith
photographs by Joel Benjamin

Can Nat, Pat, and Pam go?

Nat can. Pat can. Pam can.

Pam can go here.

Pat can, too.

Pam can read.

Pat can, too.

Pam can write.

Nat can, too.

Pam can draw.

Pat can, too.

Nat can, too.

Pam can fan! Nat can fan!
Pat can fan! We can fan!

Think About the Story

We Can!
written by Diane Hoyt-Goldsmith
photographs by Joel Benjamin

1 What can the children do at school?

2 Do you think the children like school? Why?

3 Would you like to go to their school? Why?

Describe a Character

Use punch-out letters to make a character's name. Then write one word to describe the character.

The More We Get Together

The more we get together,
  together, together,
The more we get together,
  the happier we'll be.
'Cause your friends are my friends,
  and my friends are your friends,
The more we get together,
  the happier we'll be.

Traditional

The Big Hit

Words to Know

a	big
find	hit
have	ran
one	tag
who	Tim
bat	Tip

Who can find a
big, big bat?
Can Sam?

We have one big bat.

Pat can hit.
Can Tip hit?

Can Tim tag Sam?

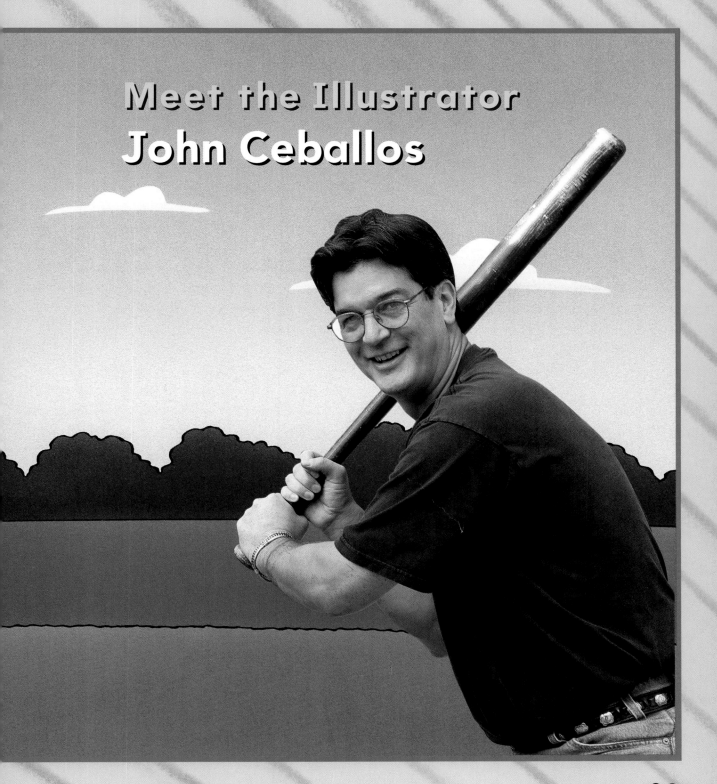

Meet the Illustrator
John Ceballos

The Big Hit

written by
Angela Shelf Medearis

illustrated by
John Ceballos

Who can find a big bat?

We have a big bat.

Who can hit?

93

We can hit!

94

Sam can hit.

Go, Sam! Sam ran.

Tim can not tag Sam.

Pat can hit.

Go, Pat! Pat ran.

99

Cam can not tag Pat.

Bam! Nat hit one big hit.

We ran, ran, ran!

Tip ran, ran, ran!

Teacher Read Aloud

Think About the Story

The **Big Hit**

written by
Angela Shelf Medearis

illustrated by
John Ceballos

1 Do you think the children like to play ball? Why?

2 Why did the children chase Tip?

3 How would you get the ball from Tip?

![Writing](pencil arrow)

Write a Name

Draw your favorite character from the story. Write the character's name.

Big Pig

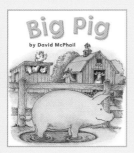

Words to Know

a	fig
find	fit
have	hat
one	pig
to	ran
who	sit
big	Tim

Who can find Big Pig?
Nan can. Can Tim?

Big Pig ran to Nan.

Sit, Big Pig.
Have one big, fat fig.

Can a hat fit Big Pig?

Meet the Author and Illustrator
David McPhail

Big Pig

by David McPhail

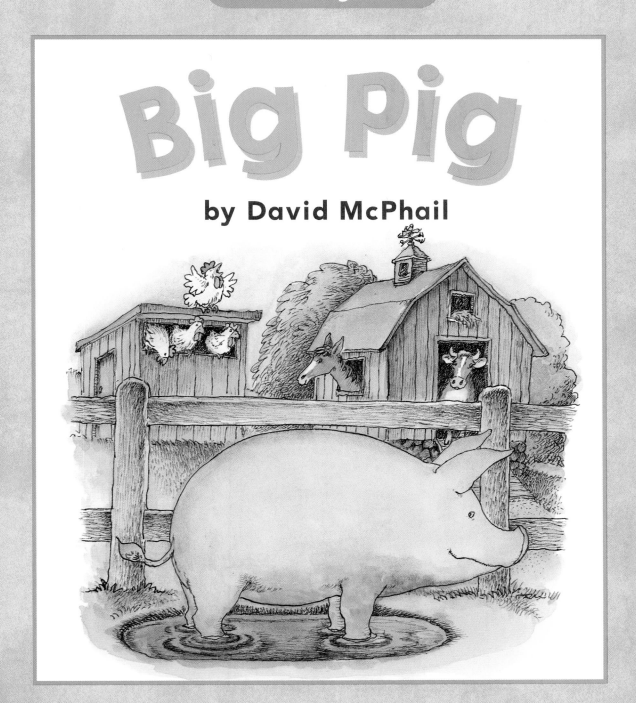

Tim can go to a farm.
Nan can, too.

Tim and Nan find a big hat.

Can the big hat fit Tim?

Can the big hat fit Nan?

Who can the big hat fit?

The big hat can fit Big Pig.

1. Feed Big Pig.
2. Sit on Big Pig.

Can Nan and Tim sit on Big Pig?

Big Pig can have one fat fig.

Nan can sit.

Big Pig can have a big carrot.

Tim can sit.

Go, Big Pig!

Big Pig ran!
Tim and Nan sat!

Think About the Story

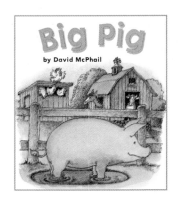

1 Why does Big Pig get the hat?

2 Why did Nan and Tim sit on Big Pig?

3 Would you like to visit Big Pig's farm? Why?

▶

Write a Menu

What does Big Pig like to eat?
Draw a picture and label it.

There Was a Small

There was a small pig who wept tears
When his mother said,
   "I'll wash your ears."
As she poured on the soap,
He cried, "Oh, how I hope
This won't happen again for ten years!"

by Arnold Lobel

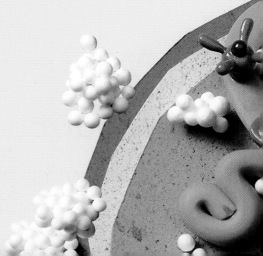

Pig Who Wept Tears

Surprise!

Teacher Read Aloud

No matter where
   I travel,
No matter where
   I roam,
No matter where
   I find myself,
I always am
   at home.

**from the poem "Riddle"
by Mary Ann Hoberman**

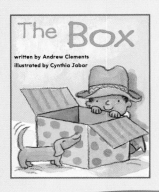

Words to Know

once	got
what	lot
box	on
Don	top
Dot	wig
fox	

Once Don and Dot got a big box. What can fit in the big box?

A wig can fit.
A fox can fit.
Can Don and Dot sit on top?

A lot can fit in the big box.

Meet the Author
Andrew Clements

Meet the Illustrator
Cynthia Jabar

The Box

written by Andrew Clements

illustrated by Cynthia Jabar

Once Don got a big box.

What can fit in the box?

One tan fox can fit.

One pig in a wig can fit.

One big hat can fit.

A lot can fit in the box.

Dot got the box.

What can Dot find in the box?

Dot can find a tan fox on top.

Dot can find a pig in a wig.

Dot can find a big hat.

Don and Dot can fit!
A lot can fit in a box!

Think About the Story

The Box
written by Andrew Clements
illustrated by Cynthia Jabar

1 How many things did Don put in the box?

2 What might Dot do with the things in the box?

3 What would you put in the box?

Write a Description

Draw something you would put in the box. Write about your picture.

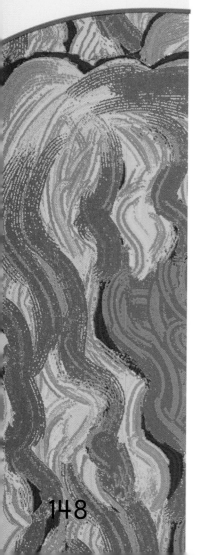

Words to Know

five	Don
four	Dot
three	Fox
two	got
upon	lot
what	Ox
box	wig
Dog	win

A big box sat upon a mat.
Can Dog win the big box?

Dog got the box!
Fox got wig one.

Ox got wig two.

Cat got wig three.

Dot got wig four.

Don got wig five.

What a lot in a big box!

Valeria Petrone

Wigs in a Box

by Valeria Petrone

A big box sat upon a shelf.
Can Pat Pig win the box?

153

Pat Pig can win.
Pat Pig can hit the ball in.

Pat Pig got the big box!
What can Pat Pig find in it?

Pat Pig can find a wig.

Pat Pig can find five wigs
in the big box!

Wig one can fit Pat Pig.

Wig two can fit Dot Fox.

Wig three can fit Don Dog.

Wig four can fit Fat Cat.

Wig five can fit Tan Ox.

Thanks a lot, Pat Pig!

Think About the Story

1. What plan did Pat Pig make when he saw the wigs in the box?

2. Why did the animals thank Pat Pig?

3. Which wig would you choose?

164

Write a Character Description

Use punch-out letters to write your favorite character's name. Then write some words to tell about the character.

Here Is

Here is the beehive.
Where are the bees?

Hidden away where
nobody sees.

Watch and you'll
see them come
out of the hive.

the Beehive

One, two, three, four, five.

Bzzzzzzzz... all fly away!

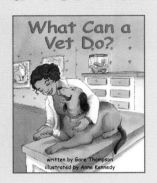

What Can a Vet Do?

written by Gare Thompson
illustrated by Anne Kennedy

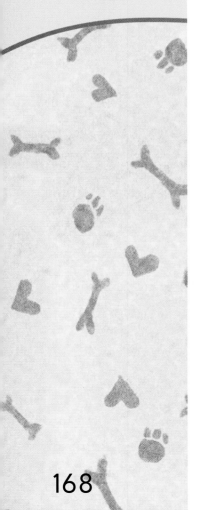

Words to Know

do	Ned
for	pen
is	pet
my	van
Ben	vet
get	wet
kit	yes

Ben is my pet.
Ben can not get wet.

Is Ben at the vet?
Ben is not at the vet yet.

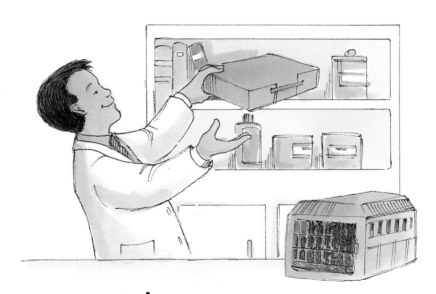

Ben can get in a pen.
A vet can get a kit.
What can a vet do for Ben?

Meet the Author
Gare Thompson

Meet the Illustrator
Anne Kennedy

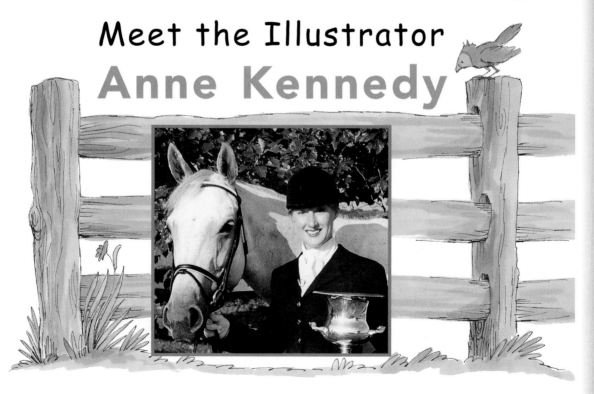

170

What Can a Vet Do?

written by Gare Thompson
illustrated by Anne Kennedy

Chapter 1

What bit my pet cat Big Ben?

Get Big Ben to the vet!

Can the vet fix Big Ben?
The vet can get a kit.

Big Ben can sit.

Big Ben can get wet.

The vet can pat Big Ben.

Yes, the vet can do a lot
for Big Ben!

Chapter 2

Ned is my big pet.
Ned is in a big pen.

Mom, get the vet!

Ned can not jump.

Here is the vet in a tan van.

The vet can get a big kit.
Can the vet fix Ned?

Yes, the vet can fix Ned!

A vet can do a lot.

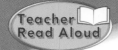
Think About the Story

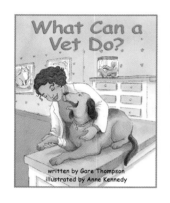

What Can a Vet Do?

written by Gare Thompson
illustrated by Anne Kennedy

1 What does a vet do?

2 How do you know the girl and the boy care about their pets?

3 Would you like to be a vet? Why?

Write a Description

Draw a picture of a pet at the vet.
Write about your picture.

Hot Fox Soup

Words to Know

I	Hen
is	kit
me	let
my	met
said	vat
you	wet
get	yes
	yet

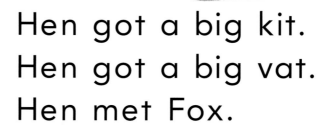

Hen got a big kit.
Hen got a big vat.
Hen met Fox.

"What can I get?" said Fox.
"You can get wet," said Hen.
"Here is my vat. Get in."
"Not me!" said Fox.

"Yes," said Hen. "Get wet!"
"Not yet!" said Fox.

Meet the Author
and Illustrator

Satoshi Kitamura

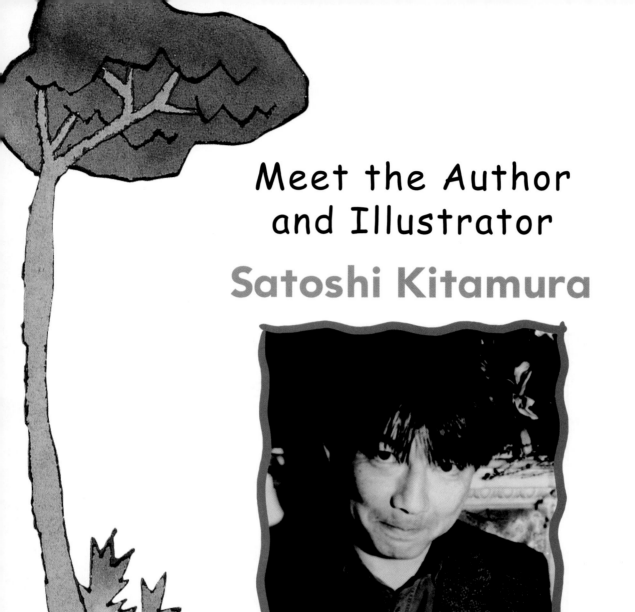

HOT FOX SOUP

by SATOSHI KITAMURA

Fox wanted hot hen soup.

Fox got a big, big vat.
Fox lit a hot, hot fire.

Fox got a noodle soup kit in a box.

Fox met Hen.
"What can I get?" said Hen.

"Get wet in my vat, Hen," said Fox.

"Not me!"
Hen ran.

Fox met Pig.

Fox wanted hot pig soup.

"What can I get?" said Pig.

"Get wet in my vat, Pig," said Fox.

"Not me!"
Pig ran.

Fox met Ox.
Fox wanted hot ox soup.

"What can I get?" said Ox.

"Get wet in my vat, Ox," said Fox.

"Not me!
I can not fit in a vat."

"Fox, you get in," said Ox.
"We can fix hot, hot fox soup!"

"Not hot fox soup!" said Fox.
"Let me fix hot, hot noodle soup."

"Is it hot yet, Fox?"

"Yes, it is hot, hot, hot," said Fox.
"Dig in!"

Think About the Story

1 Why wouldn't the animals get in Fox's vat?

2 How did Ox surprise Fox?

3 Would you eat soup with Fox? Why?

Writing ▶

Write a Sign

Make a sign with the words
Hot_____ Soup. Add your own
word to complete the sign.

Polly, Put

the Kettle On

Polly, put the kettle on,
Polly, put the kettle on,
Polly, put the kettle on,
We'll all have tea.

English Traditional Song

A Hut for Zig Bug

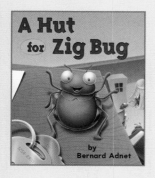

Words to Know

does	fun
he	hut
live	jug
where	quit
Bug	rug
but	up
cup	Zig

Where does Zig Bug live?
Does he live in a hut?

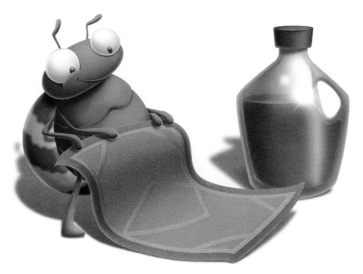

Zig Bug can get a jug.
Zig Bug can get a rug.

Do not quit!
Can Zig Bug fix up a fun hut?

Meet the Author and Illustrator
Bernard Adnet

A Hut for Zig Bug

by
Bernard Adnet

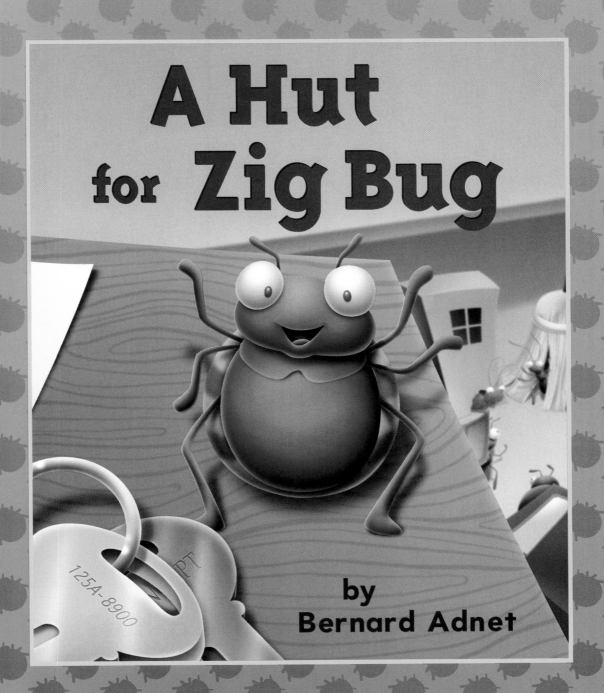

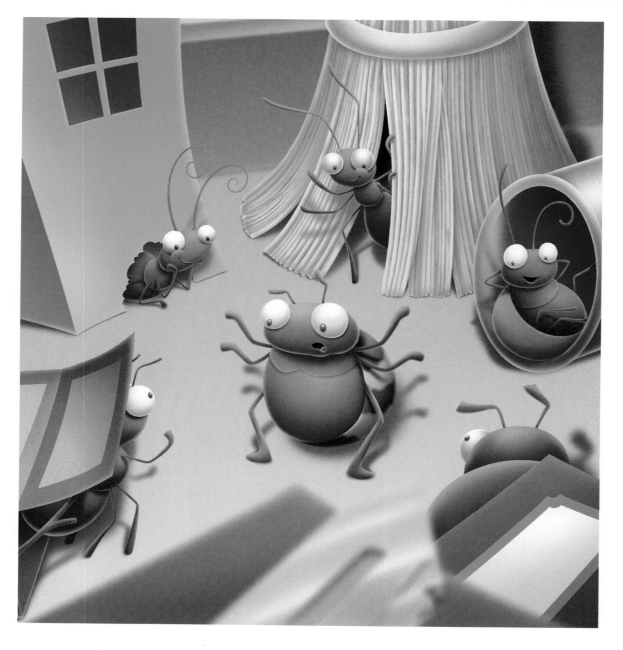

Does Zig Bug have a hut?
He does not have a hut yet.

Where can Zig Bug live?
Can he live in here?

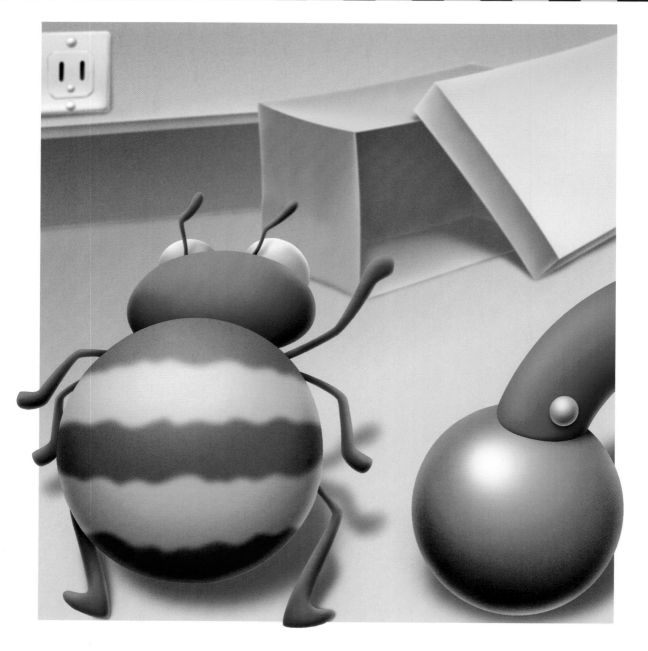

**Can Zig Bug fix a box for a hut?
Yes, he can fix up a fun hut.**

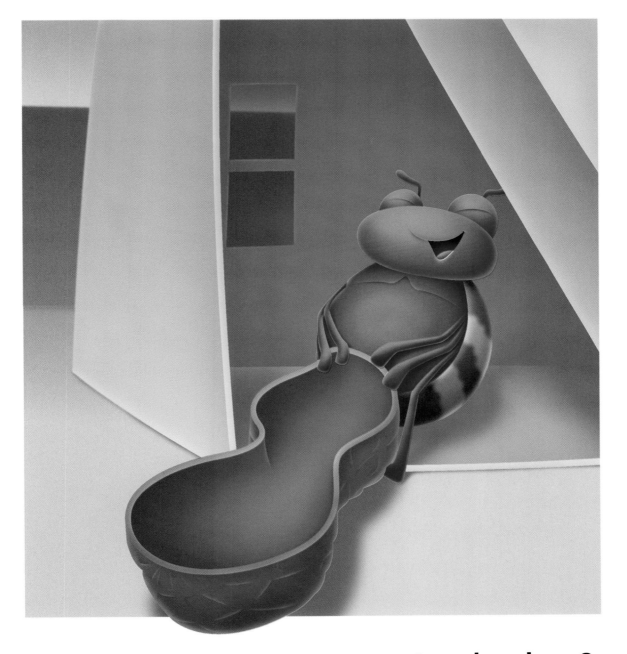

Can Zig Bug get a cot in the hut?

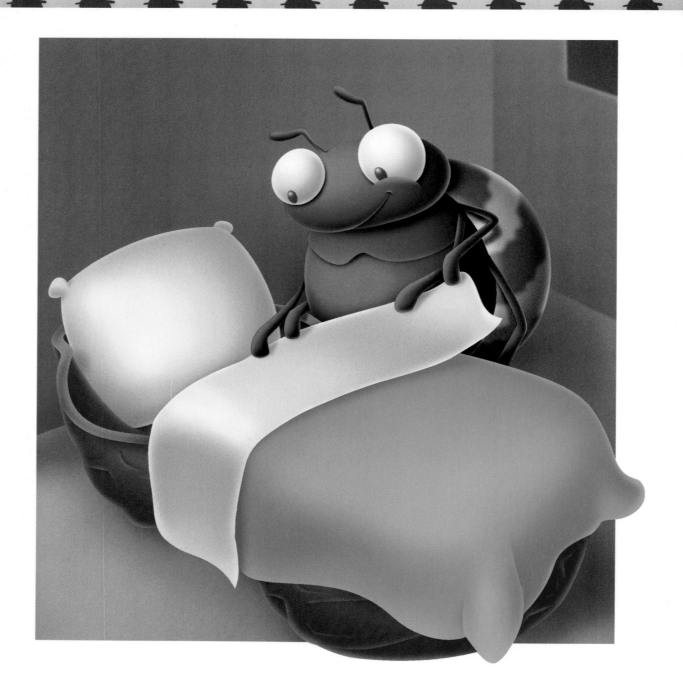

Yes, a cot can fit in the hut.

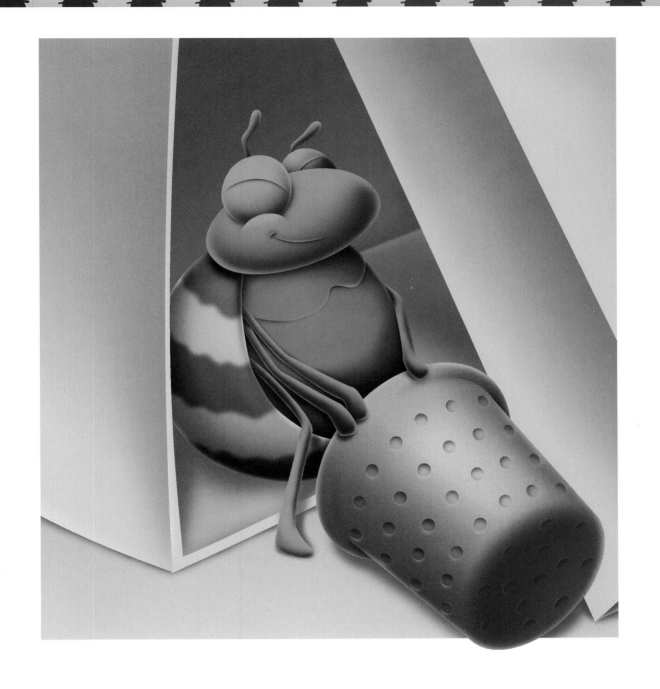

Can Zig Bug get a jug in the hut?

Yes, a jug can fit in the hut.
A cot and a jug can fit.

Can Zig Bug get a rug in the hut?

Yes, a rug can fit in the hut.
A cot, a jug, and a rug can fit.

Can Zig Bug get a cup in the hut?

Yes, a cup can fit in the hut.
A cot, a jug, a rug, and
a cup can fit.

Can Zig Bug fit in the hut?

**Do not quit, Zig Bug!
You can fit!**

Zig Bug does fit!
A cot, a jug, a rug, a cup,
and Zig Bug fit in the hut!

Think About the Story

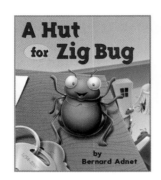

A Hut
for **Zig Bug**

by
Bernard Adnet

1 Was Zig Bug smart? Why?

2 What else could Zig Bug put in his hut?

3 Will Zig Bug be happy in his hut? Why?

Write a List

List the things Zig Bug put in his hut. Add some more things he could put in there.

Words to Know

are	but	quit
away	hut	zag
does	jig	zig
pull	run	
they	tug	

Cat is in a big hut.
Rat does not run away.
Can Rat pull Cat?

Rat said, "You are big,
but I can tug!"
They tug, tug, tug.

"I quit," said Cat.
Rat does a jig.
Zig zag, zig zag!

Meet the Author
Veronica Freeman Ellis

Meet the Artist
Mary Lynn Carson

Meet the
Photographer
Richard Haynes

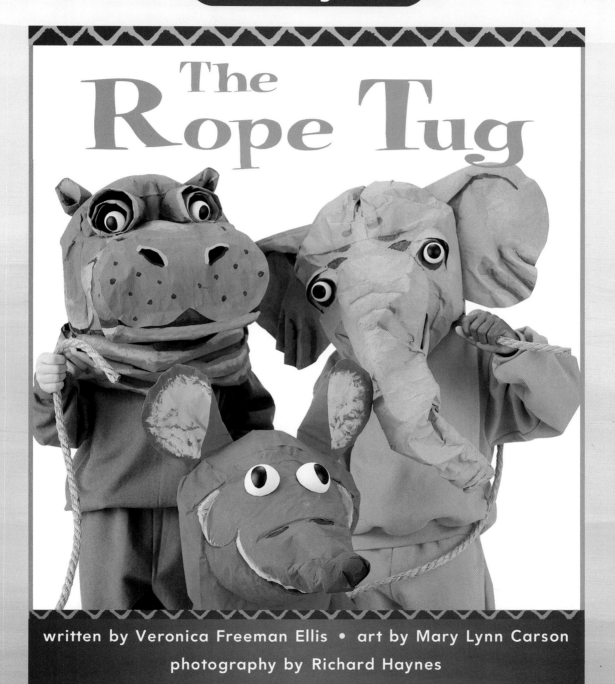

The Rope Tug

written by Veronica Freeman Ellis • art by Mary Lynn Carson

photography by Richard Haynes

Narrator

Elephant

Hippo

Rat

238

 Elephant can get in the hut.
Hippo can get in the hut.

Rat can not get in.
Rat can not fit.

Let me in! Let me in!

You can not fit, Rat.
Run away, Rat!
Run, run, run!

 I can pull you outside.
I am not big, but I can tug.

242

 You can not tug me, Rat.

 You can not tug me, Rat.

 Can you tug and pull me?
I am not big, but I can tug.

 We are big!
We can pull you!
Get a big rope, Rat!

 Rat can get a big, big rope.

 Rat can zig zag, zig zag.

 Tug, tug, tug!

 You can not win, Rat!
Tug, tug, tug!

They are big!
They tug and tug and tug,
but they can not pull Rat.

 I quit!

 I quit!

 Rat does a jig.

 I win! I win!
I'm not big, but I can tug!

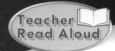
Think About the Story

1 Why wouldn't Elephant and Hippo let Rat in the hut?

2 How did Rat surprise Elephant and Hippo?

3 How else could Rat have gotten Elephant and Hippo out of the hut?

![Writing] ▶

Write a Description

Draw your favorite part of the play.
Write some words to tell about it.

Way Down South

Way down South where
bananas grow,
A grasshopper stepped on
an elephant's toe.
The elephant said, with tears
in his eyes,
"Pick on somebody your
own size."

Anonymous